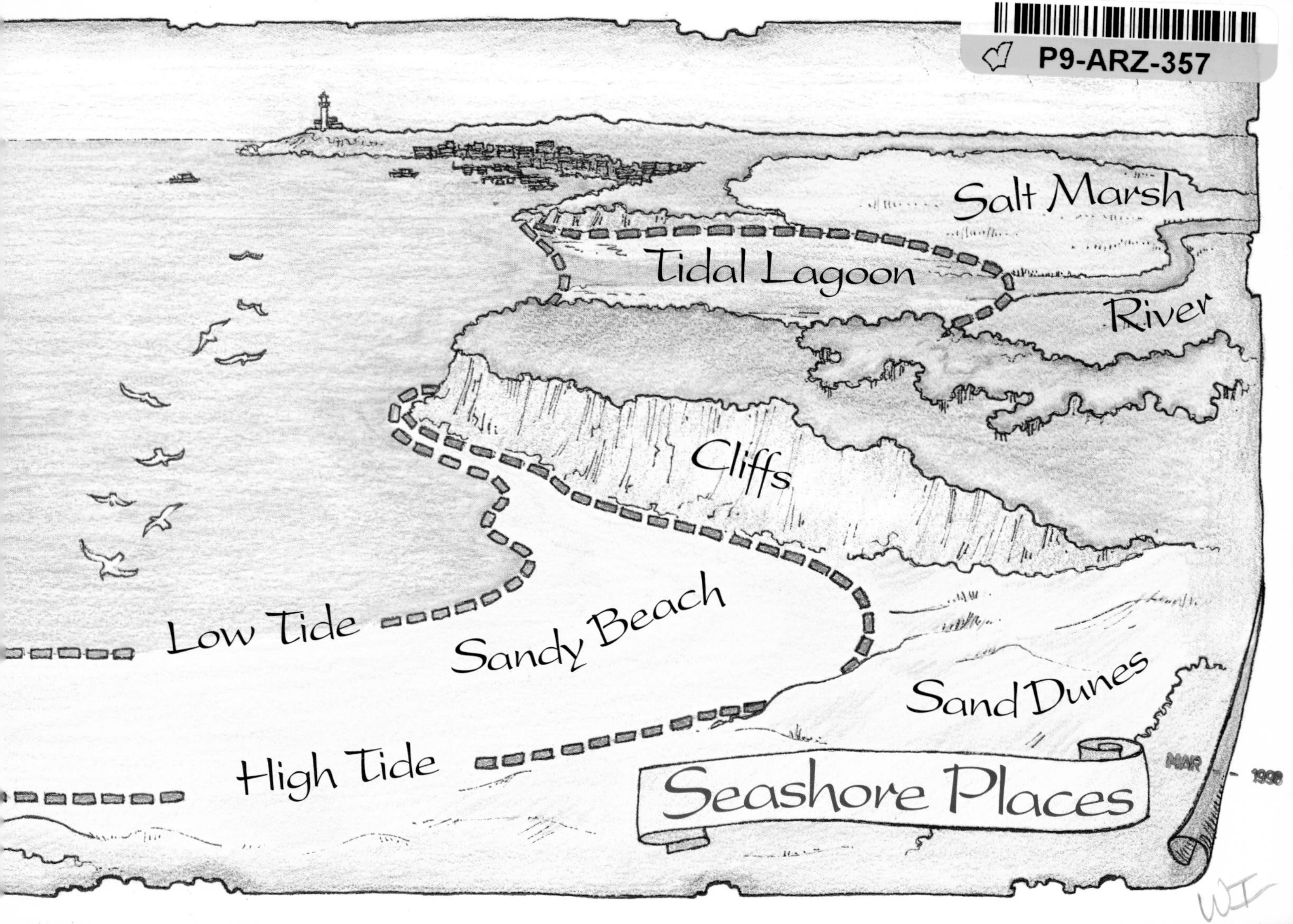

Salt Marsh

Tidal Lagoon

River

Cliffs

Low Tide

Sandy Beach

Sand Dunes

High Tide

Seashore Places

To Nathaniel Chalmer Cooper,
for later—Ann

The Wild Wonders Series is supported in part by the
Lloyd David and Carlye Cannon Wattis Foundation.

The animals and plants illustrated in this book are typical of the
Pacific Coast of North America and have been reviewed and
approved by scientists at the Denver Museum of Natural History.

We would like to thank Dr. Charles Preston, Curator of Ornithology
at the Denver Museum of Natural History, for reviewing this book.
His help and input at all stages of this project were invaluable.

Book design by Jill Soukup

International Standard Book Number 1-57098-121-2
Library of Congress Catalog Card Number 96-72308

Published by the Denver Museum of Natural History Press
2001 Colorado Boulevard, Denver, Colorado 80205
in cooperation with Roberts Rinehart Publishers
5455 Spine Road, Boulder, Colorado 80301
(303) 530-4400

Distributed in the UK and Ireland by
Roberts Rinehart Publishers
Trinity House, Charleston Road
Dublin 6, Ireland

Distributed in the U.S. and Canada by Publishers Group West

Printed in China

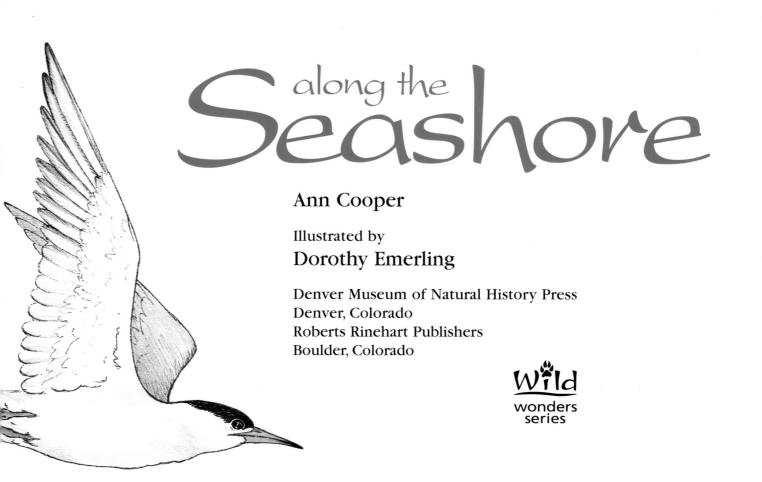

along the
Seashore

Ann Cooper

Illustrated by
Dorothy Emerling

Denver Museum of Natural History Press
Denver, Colorado
Roberts Rinehart Publishers
Boulder, Colorado

Wild
wonders
series

The Land of Tides

Tide's in! Waves swirl and froth around the rocks. The biggest waves drench cling-tight mussels and splash barnacles. Along the beach, waves nibble at the strandline and retreat again. They leave behind clues of ocean life: a pink crab claw, a fish bone, a scallop shell, and fragments of slimy seaweed.

Twice each day this between-tides area belongs to the sea. Sea creatures of the sandy beach and rocky shore feast while they can. Some catch bits of food that drift in with the waves. Others hunt and eat small animals. Danger comes from the ocean—battering waves, tumbling boulders, and seals and fish looking for dinner.

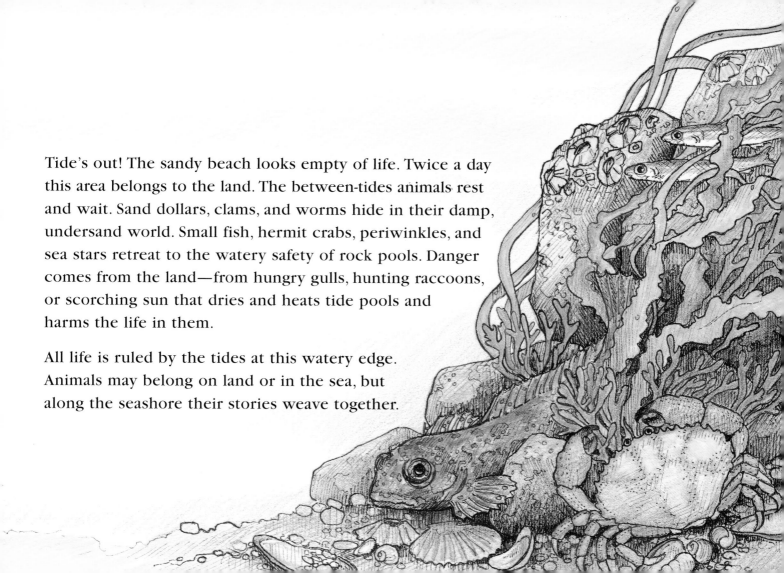

Tide's out! The sandy beach looks empty of life. Twice a day this area belongs to the land. The between-tides animals rest and wait. Sand dollars, clams, and worms hide in their damp, undersand world. Small fish, hermit crabs, periwinkles, and sea stars retreat to the watery safety of rock pools. Danger comes from the land—from hungry gulls, hunting raccoons, or scorching sun that dries and heats tide pools and harms the life in them.

All life is ruled by the tides at this watery edge. Animals may belong on land or in the sea, but along the seashore their stories weave together.

Seal's Feast

Seal lazily scratched her belly with one flipper. She felt snoozy and warm. Her pup, sleepy and full of milk, lay next to her on the sunbaked rocks, body-basking. It seemed too much trouble to slip into the cold ocean . . . until foamy waves began to slosh around her. She yawned, nuzzled her pup as if to say "Wake up," and slithered into the sea. Pup bawled pitifully, then followed his mother.

Mother Seal was hungry for fish and squid. She wanted to dive deep, to speed through the kelp in search of dinner. But she had Pup to consider. She kept Pup close, making do with shallow dives. In between, she surfaced, bobbing like a bottle, to keep watch.

A squawking mass of gulls and terns swirled above a swift tidal current. They were feeding on shoals of surface fish. Gull-fuss was a good fishing hint! Seal hurried to feast, too. Suddenly, she spotted a dark fin. Danger! Orca! Seal swam as fast as she could, her pup piggybacking. She didn't stop until they reached a narrow, barnacled cove too shallow for the whale to follow.

Snippets About Seals

Getting Around

Seals dog-paddle slowly with their front flippers, or swim fast with a fishlike wiggle, using their flippers to steer. Seals cannot walk well on land. They lumber along like giant slugs!

Deep Breath?

Seals breathe out, close their nostrils, and dive deep in search of prey. They may stay down for half an hour. Seals cannot breathe in water. If they cannot come up for air, they drown.

Food

Seals are carnivores. They eat many kinds of fish, crustaceans (crabs and shrimps), and squid.

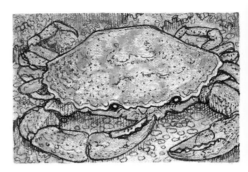

Neighbors

Seals often snooze on rocks that are awash at high tide—rocks shared by limpets, sea stars, anemones, and other between-tides animals.

Sad Seals?

Unlike us, seals do not have ducts in their eyes to drain tears. The eye-rinsing tears constantly spill down their cheeks.

Fur and Blubber

Seals' fur keeps them warm on land. Under the fur is a thick layer of blubber (fat) that keeps them warm in the water.

Babies

Seal pups (babies) are born on rocks or quiet beaches. What if the tide comes in? The pups can swim soon after they are born!

Mammals

Seals are mammals. They have fur and their born-alive pups suckle on milk. Seal milk is half fat, almost as rich as whipping cream!

Enemies

Orcas (killer whales) and sharks hunt seals. Eagles sometimes prey on seal pups.

Diving for Dinner

Weeks ago, Cormorant courted his mate for her fine, glossy-black feathers. With wings spread, he skittered across the waves to impress her. He dived for a rockweed frond, tossed and caught it. He croaked *okokokokok*, moving his head snakily. The birds touched beaks and twined necks, becoming a pair. They built a seaweed nest

at the edge of the crowded cormorant colony on a rocky sea stack. Now they had four hatched and hungry chicks, and it was Father Cormorant's turn to fish.

He flew to the rocky inlet, landed on the waves, then dived down, down to the reef. With his webbed feet he arrowed through the water without splashing. Cormorant searched, steering with his stiff tail, until he spied a shoal of silvery herrings. Spreading his wings, he almost flew underwater. He caught fish after fish in his jaggedy beak, gulping them down. Full, he splatter-splashed across the water surface until he was airborne and flew swiftly home. It was time to feed his chicks—time to rest and dry his wings.

Cormorant Facts

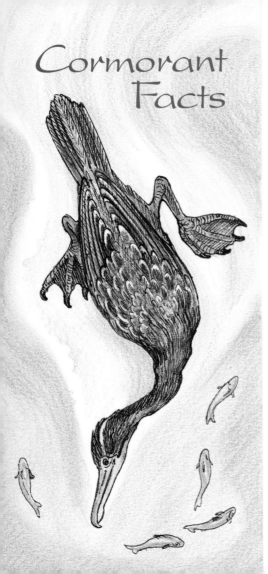

Diving Champions!

Cormorants often shallow-dive, but they *can* go down two hundred feet (that's about as deep as a twenty-story building is tall). They stay down (hold your breath!) more than a minute.

Fancy Footwork

A cormorant's webbed feet make superfast swim and dive paddles!

Fish-trap Beaks

A cormorant's hooked beak has saw-blade edges to grip slimy fish.

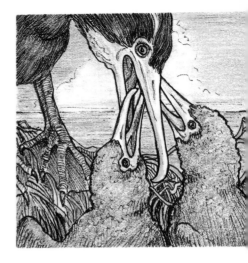

Food

Adult cormorants eat small fish, shrimps, crabs, and shellfish.

A parent feeds chicks a diet of mushy, partly digested fish that drips from the parent's beak. A chick sticks its head into its parent's mouth to beg for food!

Friend or Foe?

Cormorants nest on cliffs and islands with other birds—murres, guillemots, and gulls—but gulls aren't very neighborly! They steal eggs and chicks to eat, and sometimes snatch a cormorant's fish catch!

Feathers

On land, cormorants often "hang out" their wings to dry. They have too little oil on their feathers to keep them completely waterproof after many dives.

Cormorants even drape their wings on rainy days. Maybe it gives them "elbow room" so they don't feel crowded and can fly away easily without bumping wings.

Nifty Nests

Cormorants build nests in trees or on rocky cliffs or islands. Besides sticks and seaweed, they build with strange "found" items. Birds trimmed one nest with combs, hairpins, and pocketknives from a deepwater shipwreck!

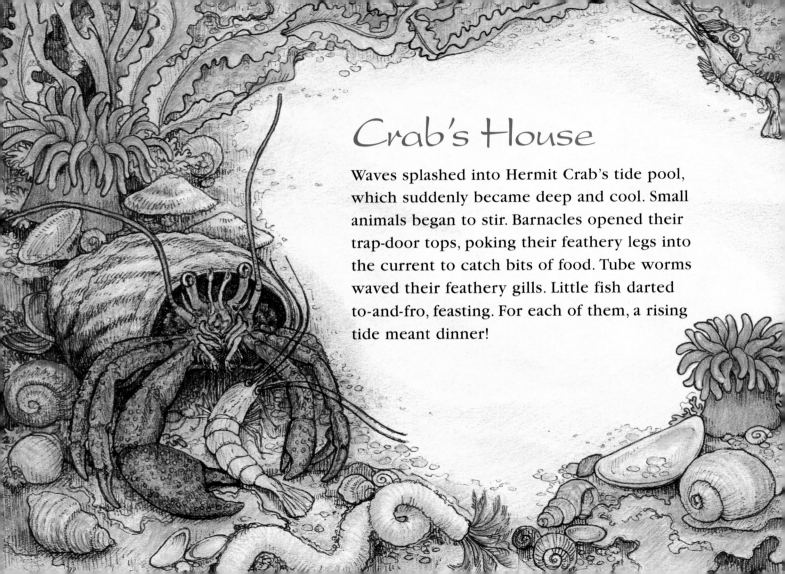

Crab's House

Waves splashed into Hermit Crab's tide pool, which suddenly became deep and cool. Small animals began to stir. Barnacles opened their trap-door tops, poking their feathery legs into the current to catch bits of food. Tube worms waved their feathery gills. Little fish darted to-and-fro, feasting. For each of them, a rising tide meant dinner!

Hermit Crab had something more important to do than eat! Her house was too tight. Before she ate another bite, she needed to find a new shell to live in—a larger one! The first shell she found was too small. The second shell was full of snail. The third shell had a pinkish purple claw-door! It already belonged to a large hermit crab.

At last, she found an empty shell. She tested it to be sure it was the right size. She wriggled her soft, curly abdomen backward into the inside spirals of the shell, and clung tight. Perfect! In this fine, roomy home, Hermit Crab had growing space. Hungry after her dangerous house-moving, she scuttled off in search of shrimps, worms, and other meaty bits to eat.

About Hermit Crabs

Fancy Homes

Hermit crab shells are sometimes covered with sponges, barnacles, or tiny anemones taking a free ride. The hitchhikers feast on food the crab drops. The crab wears a disguise!

Legs

A hermit crab's right claw is the larger one and acts like a front door! Its left claw tears up food. It has four walking legs and four clinging-to-home legs.

Neighbors

Many animals share the tide pool world: seabirds, fish, shrimps, crabs, sea stars, limpets, chitons, worms, and sponges (yes, they're animals!).

Enemies

Many seabirds, fish, sea anemones, and other crabs eat hermit crabs.

Food

Hermit crabs eat tiny worms, shrimps, and other animals—dead or alive. They also eat bits of seaweed plants.

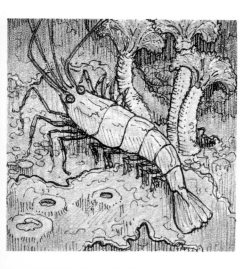

Families

After mating, a female hermit crab lays masses of orange eggs. She holds them inside her mobile home to keep them safe. After they hatch, larvae (young) swim free until their first molt (skin-shedding). Then each one finds a shell-home of its own.

Skeleton

A hermit crab has an exoskeleton (outside skeleton) covering the front of its body. But its tail is squishy, so it lives in a found shell.

All crabs shed their too tight exoskeletons as they grow. Underneath are new shells waiting to harden after the crabs have a growing spurt.

Raccoon's Surprises

Raccoon woke from her day's sleep and clambered down from her tree den beyond the dunes. *Sniff, snuffle, sniff.* A delicious salty, seaside, low-tide smell drifted on the breeze. Seafood tonight? That would be a tasty change! Raccoon pitter-pattered through the dune grasses onto the beach. She poked around in a few tide pools, feeling with her

sensitive paws. She nosed along the strandline, scrabbling for anything the sea had left behind. A fish, a dead bird, a few clams, a mole crab—she wasn't fussy. She'd eat anything!

Ouch! Not smart! Something from under a hump of washed-up kelp fastened onto her nose. The sharp, pinching claws made her whiskers quiver. She shook her head this way and that, but the crab held tight. Raccoon pawed at the crab. She didn't like being grabbed by her dinner! *Splosh!* Raccoon was so distracted by the crab, she didn't notice the large wave breaking behind her. Bedraggled, dripping, and hungry, she pitter-pattered back to the salt marsh. She left behind only a trail of paw prints and a crab scuttling sideways to safety.

Seaside Raccoons

First Outing
Baby raccoons stay in the den until they are about eight weeks old. Then they go out each night with their mother to search for food.

Copycats?
Young raccoons learn food-finding skills by copying their mother as she digs for clams, turtle eggs, and other tasty tidbits.

Enemies
Dogs, coyotes, eagles, and owls may catch raccoons, but raccoons fight back with their sharp teeth and claws.

Stop, Thief!
Sandpipers and terns make ground nests in the dunes. Raccoons raid the nests and steal eggs and chicks. They will take gull and cormorant eggs, too, if they can get to the colonies.

Hold Tight!

Beach and rocky-shore animals must hold tight against battering waves. Mussels make tough, tie-down threads. Limpets cling on with strong foot muscles. Urchins wedge tight in rocks with spiky spines. Barnacles stick to rocks with barnacle glue.

Even so, small creatures get dislodged by storms or predators and end up as food for hungry scavengers.

Neighbors

Many mammals and birds besides raccoons forage on the dunes and beach: skunks, foxes, mink, rats, mice, gulls, and crows.

Washing Food?

Raccoons have paws like little hands. They feel for prey in the water with delicate scrabbling. It may look as if they were washing their food. But they are just as likely to eat dirty food straight from the trash! They'll eat almost anything!

Gone Fishin'

A stiff breeze blew in from the ocean, tumbling the waves and swirling dry sand from the dunes. This was a day to fish in the calm waters of the sheltered lagoon. Osprey circled high, flapping and gliding, watching . . . for the silvery flash of a darting fish. He was hungry, but he wasn't fishing only for himself. He had other mouths—his mate and three hungry nestlings—to feed.

With a shimmer and a ripple, a fish flickered in the shallows. Osprey plunged. *Whoosh!* He thrust his talons forward, flung his wings back, and grasped the fish. *Splash!* Water splattered high into the air. From the force of his plunge and with the weight of his fine catch, Osprey sank below the surface for a moment. Flapping his powerful wings, he pulled himself free and rose into the air.

He rearranged the large fish as he flew. It was easier to fly—more streamlined—when the fish's head pointed forward. Then Osprey headed home. His mate waited in their high lookout nest in a bare snag, her wings spread slightly to shelter her chicks. *Chirchirchirchir,* she greeted her mate softly, as if to say "Thanks for dinner!"

More About Ospreys

Eggs

A mother osprey usually lays three eggs. They are cinnamon or pink with brown blotches.

Families

Osprey chicks hatch in about five weeks, and keep the parents busy. The mother guards and the father hunts. The first hatched chick gets more food and grows the fastest—and fattest!

Talons

Ospreys grip fishy prey with their long, curved talons and rough toes.

Splash!

Ospreys see fish from high above the lagoon, river, or ocean. Then they dive for them. Splash! Things in water are not where they seem to be, because of the way light rays work. But ospreys allow for this when they grab for their prey.

Winter

Ospreys migrate south in winter and return to their stick nests in spring. They use the nests year after year, adding new sticks until the nests are huge.

Food

Ospreys, also known as fish hawks, eat herrings, perch, pike, salmon, eels, and other fish. When fish are scarce, they hunt small birds, mice, snakes, and frogs.

Enemies

Ospreys have very few enemies, except for bald eagles, which may steal their fish catch or even take over their nests.

Neighbors

Other birds share the tidal lagoon, salt marsh, and river inlet, including ducks, herons, egrets, and kingfishers.

Sea Star's Journey

A swift surge of cool, fresh wave splashed through the narrow channel. Sea Star held tight against the crashing and pounding, waiting to be properly underwater again. That was when Sea Star would clamber up to the mussel beds to feast. Urchin was on the move, too. It crept on its long spines. It grazed seaweed and slime, trusting its spines would keep it safe from ocean enemies swooshing in for fast food.

The waves washed the grains of sand away from Anemone's jelly-blob body. Anemone opened like a fancy flower. Its deadly tentacles streamed out into the current, ready with poisonous stinging cells to catch any tiny shrimps or other food that swept by. Sea Star tube-footed its way over Anemone, not bothered by the stinging tentacles. They would not harm Sea Star's knobby body.

Sea Star traveled slowly over the rocks, grabbing with a leading arm, letting go with a trailing arm. The mussels were open and feeding, but clamped shut when Sea Star came near. Sea Star humped over one of them, gripped the shell halves with two of its arms and pulled . . . and pulled . . . and pulled. Soon the mussel got tired, straining to stay closed. Its shell gaped and Sea Star squeezed its stomach inside the mussel and ate.

Rock Pool Residents

Anemone's Enemy

(Say that fast!) Nudibranchs eat small anemones, stinging cells and all! Nudibranchs do not digest poison cells. They store them as weapons to protect their own bodies.

Anemone Young

Anemones make new anemones in three ways. Some split to make two. Some grow "buds" (tiny anemones) around their bases. Some hatch free-swimming larvae (young) that end up finding far-off rocks to settle on.

"Flower" Animals

Anemones seem more like plants than animals. Mostly they stay put and wait for food to arrive.

What a Mouth!

An anemone is like a sack with a drawstring. Its mouth is in the middle of a ring of tentacles. Food goes in, and leftover bits come out of the same hole.

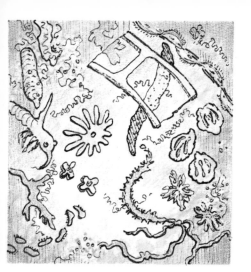

Plankton

Seawater contains
millions of tiny drifting
plants and animals called
plankton. Larvae of crabs,
shrimps, sea stars, jellyfish,
anemones, and urchins
count as plankton. Lots
of them get eaten.

Echinoderms

Sea stars and urchins
are echinoderms (spiny-
skinned animals).

Any Foot Forward

Any way can be forward
for a sea star. It has no
front or back. Sea stars
have rows of gripping
tube feet on their arms
for walking, clinging,
and feeding.

Enemies of Urchins

Gulls are not put off by
urchin spines. They catch
urchins, carry them high
in the air, and drop them
to smash open on rocks.
Then they eat the urchins'
squishy insides.

Dolphin's Baby

For months, Dolphin swam with her herd, skimming
the waves as she hunted for fish and squid to eat.
Click-click-click, she'd call, listening for *click-click*
echoes that told her where to find the shoals of
smelt and anchovies. She rode the bow waves
ahead of fishing boats way out in the bay. As she
leaped, sleek and streamlined, Dolphin felt strong
and ready. For nearly a year, her baby had been
growing inside her body. Now it was time . . .

Dolphin "aunties" (other females) swam close by, keeping watch. They would warn Dolphin of sharks and other dangers and help her and her baby if need be. Dolphin wriggled her smooth, fishlike form. Her baby began to squeeze out of a special slit in her body. He came tail first into the ocean. Quickly, Mother Dolphin nudged him upward. Hurry! Hurry! She shoved him to the surface so he could open his blowhole and take his first breath of air. Then she bit the cord that still joined their bodies.

Her baby! Her breathing, swimming, diving baby! He must be hungry for his first milky meal! As they bobbed together in the waves, Dolphin squirted rich, fatty milk from her nipples into her baby's mouth.

Dolphin Details

Breathing

Dolphins breathe air through their head-top blowholes, which are modified nostrils that can close underwater.

Teeth

Dolphins have about two hundred sharp, pointed, back-slanted teeth to grip their slippery prey.

Whale Whiskers

Unlike seals, dolphins and whales do not have fur. Some have a few whiskers, that's all! They keep warm with layers of underskin blubber.

Porpoise? Dolphin?

Porpoises have rounded heads; dolphins have foreheads and "beaks." Both swim like fish, but they are mammals and milk-feed their young underwater! Babies drink squirted milk so they don't have to suck—and get saltwater, too.

Fishing Party

Dolphins hunt in herds of hundreds. Their click calls and wild swimming panic fish shoals so they are easier to catch. Dolphins hunt where currents full of plankton swirl up. Fish and squid gather to feed on the plankton—and dolphins gather to feast on them!

Neighbors

When fishing is good, whales, dolphins, seals, porpoises, sea lions, gulls, jaegers, and terns enjoy the feast together.

Enemies

Sharks, orcas, and false killer whales are natural predators of dolphins. Humans also kill some dolphins by accident when the dolphins get caught in fishing nets and drown.

Beached

No one knows why dolphins and whales sometimes wash up on beaches and die. They may be old or sick, and too weak to come up for air. Or they may be chasing prey too fast to watch (or hear!) where they are going.

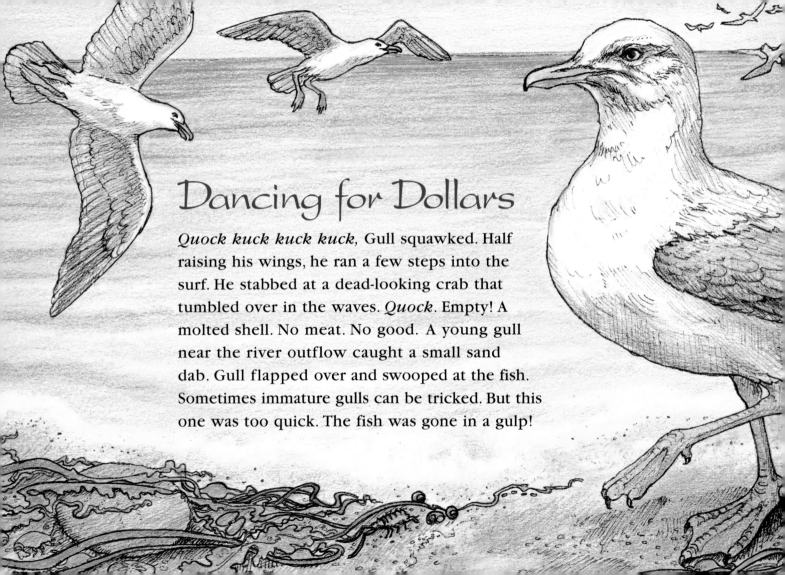

Dancing for Dollars

Quock kuck kuck kuck, Gull squawked. Half raising his wings, he ran a few steps into the surf. He stabbed at a dead-looking crab that tumbled over in the waves. *Quock.* Empty! A molted shell. No meat. No good. A young gull near the river outflow caught a small sand dab. Gull flapped over and swooped at the fish. Sometimes immature gulls can be tricked. But this one was too quick. The fish was gone in a gulp!

No easy meal today! Gull began to tread the sand as the waves dropped back. He stepped from foot to foot as if he were performing a strange dance, puddling the wet sand. It worked perfectly. A small clam rose to the surface. Gull gobbled it up. A worm, a mole crab, then another larger clam came up. Gull ate them, too. Gull's beak was strong for eating shellfish, but sometimes he needed to smash them open on the rocks.

Then Gull found a sand dollar. A few pecks and he splintered its flat shell to reach the sweet, meaty insides. Full at last, Gull burped up a pinkish pellet full of crab-shell fragments that he couldn't digest. He'd eaten well today!

Gull Facts

Chicks

A gull's eggs take about thirty days to hatch. Chicks stay in the nest until their fuzz dries— a few hours. Then they move about, returning to tuck under the parent in the nest for warmth, shade, and safety, or "freezing" when danger threatens.

Hungry! Hungry!

Chicks know by instinct to peck at the red dot on a parent's beak to ask for food. The parent gets the message and regurgitates (burps up) food for them.

Food

Gulls eat fish, shellfish, urchins, and anything they can scavenge from tide pools, the beach, or the strandline. They steal fish from cormorants and pelicans, and eggs from birds nesting in nearby colonies. They follow fishing boats for garbage thrown overboard.

Sand Dollars

These pancake-shaped sea urchins live in sand. Their tube feet make five-petal patterns on top of their tests (shells). They have feeding channels leading to round mouth holes on their undersides.

Dangers

Like all seabirds, gulls are harmed by oil spills, pollution, and trash.

Nesting

Gulls build ground nests in noisy colonies on islands, sea stacks, or undisturbed beaches.

Neighbors

Like gulls, sanderlings (small shorebirds) poke and pry for clams and worms along the wave line. They run away like windup toys as the waves advance.

In the Sand

A beach may look flat and empty, but all sorts of animals live under the sand. That is how they stay damp when the tide goes out.

A Fishy Tale

Long strands of seaweed swayed in the swell of the waves. They were like the leaves and branches of a towering undersea forest. A school of silvery anchovies darted in and out of the strands near the surface. Sea Trout rushed at a bite-size one. Turning as if the shoal were one body, the anchovies shimmered like sunlight on ripples. The flickers and flashes confused Sea Trout. He missed his catch.

Sea Trout did not dare take too much time chasing the little fish. He had other things to do. He had to guard the cluster of brilliant blue eggs that his female had laid on the rocks. Between short forays to catch a shrimp or chase after fish, he darted back to the rocks to make sure his eggs were safe. Until they hatched, the eggs were his responsibility. It would not do for a foraging crab to gobble up his young-to-be.

Sea Trout was wary for himself, too. He kept a wide eye open for lurking predators—above and below. He watched for the shadowy shapes of torpedo rays and the lumpy, finny shapes of camouflaged enemies. He must be ever alert in his dangerous, underwater-jungle home.

Fishy Facts

Fish-eye View

Most fish have eyes on the sides of their head, which allows them to see forward, sideways, and almost backward.

Flounders

Flounder fish are flat and camouflaged. They lie on one side and both their eyes look upward. They look like sand or pebbles until they ripple away with frilly fins.

Getting Air

Fish breathe with gills, special flaps with good blood supply that take oxygen from water.

Do Fish Sleep?

Fish have no eyelids to close. You can't tell if they're asleep. Hidden in rock crevices or kelp, they take a trance break.

Scales

Fish scales are like flexible armor. They protect a fish's body.

Zap!

A torpedo ray's skin is covered with toothlike scales that feel like sandpaper. A ray makes electricity using special muscles and nerves in its body. It stuns its prey with a large jolt. Zap!

Schools

Fish schools (groups of fish swimming together for safety) have nothing to do with classes or learning anything!

Fish Millions

Many fish lay hundreds to millions of eggs and give them no care. A few survive. Other fish bear live young—a surer start in life!

Enemies

Sea mammals, birds, octopuses, crabs, sea stars, and many other land and sea animals eat fish.

Pelicans . . .

dive—splash!—to catch fish in their incredible, expandable throat pouches.

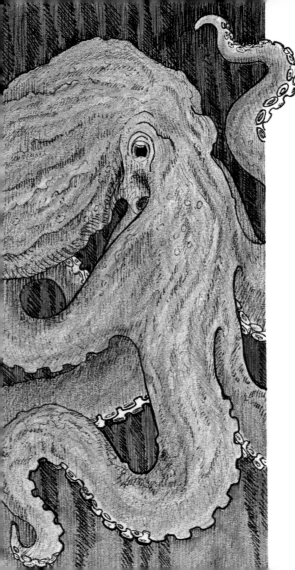

Animals All Around

Each rock, cliff, sea stack, dune, and beach shelters countless creatures. Anywhere you go, there are more animals around than you see. Which of these other seashore animals did you find as you read the story?

Octopuses

Octopuses eat crabs, scallops, mussels, clams, worms, and fish. They catch prey with their eight arms, which are covered with rows of grab-tight suckers. Octopuses escape their enemies by squirting out water and jetting backward.

Scallops

To escape enemies, a scallop closes its two hinged shells so fast that the jet of water shoots it to safety.

Jellyfish

Jellyfish drift in the sea with pulsing, open-close body movements. Their stinging tentacles trail below to catch prey.

Orcas

Orcas (killer whales) are the largest dolphins. They echolocate prey by sending out clicking sounds and listening for bounce-back echoes.

Humpback Whales

Instead of teeth, these whales have baleen (huge, hanging strainers) in their mouths. They strain tons of plankton out of the water to eat.

Did You Find?

Porpoise
Mink
Pelican
Heron
Tern
Shark
Ray
Flounder
Urchin
Sand dollar
Lobster
Shrimp
Crab
Barnacle
Tube worm
Mussel
Nudibranch

What Kind of Animal?

Many kinds of animal share the seashore habitat. The story animals belong to these groups:

▲ Birds have feathers and lay eggs with hard shells from which their chicks hatch.

▲ Mammals have hair (at least a whisker or two!) and feed their born-alive babies on milk.

▲ Invertebrates have no backbone. They may have shells, spiny skin, or be soft and jellylike.

▲ Fish have backbones and scales. They live in water and breathe through gills.

Tracks

Did you notice tracks on some pages? They are life-size. Measure them with your hand to test the size of the animals' feet.

Treasure Maps

Front map: Find the rocks where Seal and her baby basked. Find the beach where Gull danced for dollars.

Back map: Which animal uses the smallest space? Who might nest on the cliffs or sea stacks? Who stays out to sea?

Dinnertime

Animals eat in different ways. Do you remember which animal fed in which way?
• Who pulled mussels open with its arms?
• Who smashed urchins on the rocks?
• Who grabbed fish with sharp talons?
• Who drank squirted milk underwater?

Strandline

Did you wonder what Raccoon found along the strandline? She found these things:

Cockleshell

Chiton

Beach Flea

Limpets

Sea Urchin Test

Mole Crab

Coquina Shell

Brittle Star

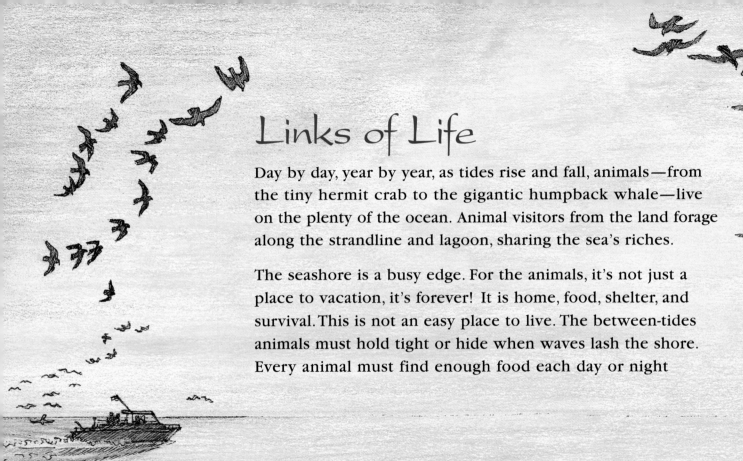

Links of Life

Day by day, year by year, as tides rise and fall, animals—from the tiny hermit crab to the gigantic humpback whale—live on the plenty of the ocean. Animal visitors from the land forage along the strandline and lagoon, sharing the sea's riches.

The seashore is a busy edge. For the animals, it's not just a place to vacation, it's forever! It is home, food, shelter, and survival. This is not an easy place to live. The between-tides animals must hold tight or hide when waves lash the shore. Every animal must find enough food each day or night

without becoming food for a larger animal. If they are lucky, the animals survive to have young.

A seal's one baby, the osprey's chicks, and the sea trout's thousands of eggs become part of the community of the seashore. No animal lives its life apart and alone. Whether the animal is hunter or hunted, small or large, each one is equally important to the way things work. Each one is a shining thread that helps weave the tapestry of nature.

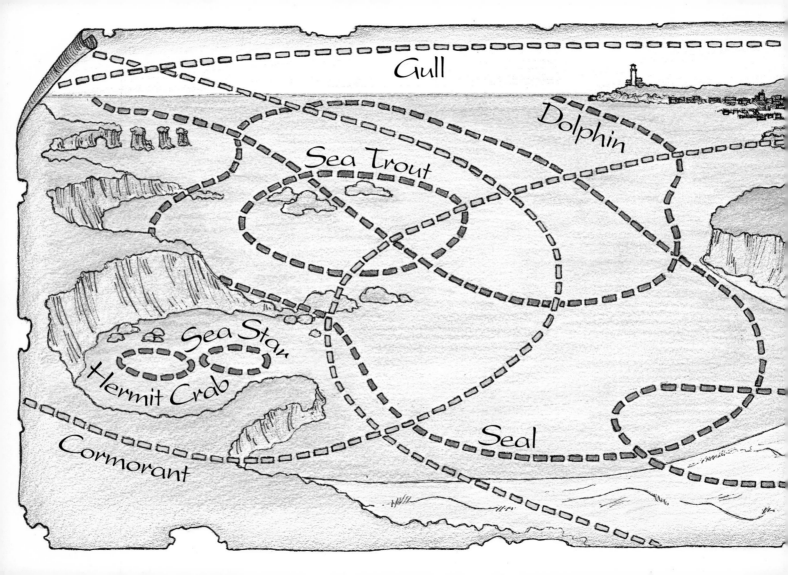